CW01512878

Original title:
Velveteen Wisps About the Elf Hook

Copyright © 2025 Swan Charm
All rights reserved.

Author: Sara Säde
ISBN HARDBACK: 978-1-80563-420-1
ISBN PAPERBACK: 978-1-80564-941-0

Glimmers of Reality Beyond the Veil

In twilight's hush, where whispers dwell,
The ancient woods hold secrets well,
Beneath the boughs, a magic breathes,
Awakening dreams like autumn leaves.

Through silver mist, the shadows dance,
Unseen forces weave a chance,
The veil between the worlds grows thin,
A flicker of what might have been.

With every step, the heartbeats sync,
In hidden realms where thoughts can think,
Each echo sings of paths unheard,
In every silence, magic stirred.

Glimmers of truth in starlit skies,
Where curiosity never dies,
A tapestry of fate unfurls,
Connecting souls from distant worlds.

So take a breath, embrace the night,
For wonders hide in plainest sight,
And as you wander, keep in mind,
Reality's veil is oft unconfined.

The Allure of Forgotten Realms

In shadows deep where wonders hide,
Ancient tales in whispers glide.
A lantern's glow, a will-o'-the-wisp,
Enticing hearts with a gentle lisp.

Forgotten paths where starlight weaves,
Ember dreams in rustling leaves.
Echoes call through the hallowed glade,
In time's embrace, the past won't fade.

Cloaked in mist, the secrets sing,
A dance of fate in the moon's soft ring.
With every step on this mysterious ground,
The allure of the lost can always be found.

Whispers of Timeless Seasons

Autumn's breath, a fiery glow,
Silent dreams in the breezes flow.
Winter's frost, a crystal fair,
Hides the warmth of tender care.

Spring awakens with a gentle sigh,
Life unfurls beneath the sky.
Summer hums with a golden tune,
Beneath the sun, in full bloom.

Each season holds a tale to share,
In nature's grasp, a whispered prayer.
Embracing change, the heart learns well,
In time's own rhythm, all stories dwell.

Secrets Unraveled in the Sylvan Night

Beneath the boughs, where shadows crawl,
The night reveals its sacred call.
A silver thread through tangled trees,
Where the moonlight dances with the breeze.

Crickets sing their twilight song,
In this realm where dreams belong.
The rustling leaves in secret speak,
Of hidden paths and spirits sleek.

With a heart so light and spirit free,
The sylvan night holds mystery.
In nature's lap, the secrets sway,
Unraveled truths beneath the lay.

Ethereal Bonds of Nature's Kin

In glades where kinship intertwines,
The threads of life in harmony signs.
Each creature small, with tales to weave,
In nature's arms, they gently leave.

Roots entwined 'neath the ancient trees,
Whispers carried by the cosmic breeze.
Every leaf, a story spun,
Of laughter, grief, and battles won.

Through petals soft and rivers wide,
Love transcends the worlds that bide.
In stillness shared, the bonds remain,
Ethereal kinship through joy and pain.

Sprites and Shadows in Celestial Muse

In the veil of night they dance,
Sprites abound in twinkling chance.
Shadows flutter, soft and light,
Guiding dreams in moon's sweet flight.

Whispers weave through ancient trees,
Magic stirs on gentle breeze.
Celestial sparkles paint the skies,
Where wonder dwells in hidden sighs.

Laughter lingers on the air,
Every secret, light as prayer.
They flutter forth with carefree grace,
In the dark, their smiles embrace.

Underneath the stars they play,
Chasing night and bright array.
In the silence, stories bloom,
In their hearts, the silent room.

From the woods, a glowing call,
Enchanted echoes, sweet and small.
Sprites and shadows, hand in hand,
In celestial realms, they stand.

The Melody of Twilight's Caress

As the sun dips low and sighs,
Twilight paints the velvet skies.
A melody begins to rise,
Hushed whispers of the night's surprise.

Crickets chirp their serenade,
In the glen, a magic made.
Moonlit paths where spirits roam,
The earth awakens, finds its home.

Soft caress of evening's calm,
Wrapping all in nature's balm.
Stars emerge with glistening tear,
Songs of twilight, pure and clear.

Fingers brush against the dew,
Dreams take flight in colors new.
Faintest glimmers guide the way,
In the arms of night, we stay.

With each note, the world transforms,
In boundless realms, our hearts conform.
Twilight's magic never ends,
In its charm, our spirit bends.

Flourish of Magic in the Dim-lit Path

In a world where shadows hide,
Magic flows like a gentle tide.
Dim-lit paths of secrets keep,
Where whispered wonders softly seep.

Twinkling lights in endless dreams,
Flowing like the starlit streams.
Every shiver of the night,
Holds the promise of delight.

Through the gloom, a voice does sing,
Echoes held in twilight's wing.
Flourish blooms at every turn,
In the heart, a fire burns.

Steps lead onward, soft and slow,
Where the hidden beckons low.
With each breath, the magic grows,
On this path, our spirit flows.

In the shadows, stories twine,
In the dim, the heart will shine.
Every turn, a tale imbued,
On the path, our souls renewed.

Echoing Crickets and the Elfin Breeze

In the hush of evening's glow,
Crickets sing, a song they sow.
Elfin breezes weave the night,
In their dance, the world feels right.

Through the grasses, whispers play,
Nature's chorus leads the way.
Beneath the stars, a magic thrums,
In every heart, the longing comes.

Glimmers of the past unfold,
Stories whispered, brave and bold.
Echoes chase the fleeting time,
In the air, both light and rhyme.

Crickets call with secret tune,
Beneath the watchful, wistful moon.
Elfin laughter in the breeze,
Dancing softly through the trees.

As the night begins to fade,
Memories of magic made.
In our dreams, forever stays,
Echoing crickets sing their praise.

The Glistening Traces of Forgotten Myths

In shadows deep where whispers throng,
The echoes of the past grow strong.
Myths twinkle softly, lost and free,
Like silver threads in tapestry.

Old spirits dance in twilight's veil,
Their stories weave a timeless tale.
With every heartbeat, memories sweep,
In glistening traces, worlds we keep.

From ancient woods to distant shore,
Forgotten tales that we restore.
A whispered name, a call to see,
The magic lingers, wild and free.

In every stone and winding brook,
The past resides, if we but look.
Through tangled roots, the secrets flow,
Of glistening paths we long to know.

Celestial Nocturne of the Woodland Spirits

Beneath the stars, in moonlit grace,
The woodland spirits find their place.
They hum a tune of soft delight,
A nocturne sung by silver light.

With shadows deep and laughter bright,
They weave the fabric of the night.
Their voices blend with rustling leaves,
In harmony where magic weaves.

The trees, they sway, as if in trance,
And ancient roots begin to dance.
A celestial symphony they weave,
For those who wander, and believe.

Each star above, a twinkling eye,
Watches over the forest nigh.
In every glade, a spirit stirs,
In whispered winds, their laughter purrs.

Dreamweavers in the Heart of the Glade

In the heart of the glade, where time stands still,
The dreamweavers weave with gentle will.
With gossamer threads of hope and fear,
They craft the visions that draw us near.

Each flicker of light, each shadow cast,
Holds a story from futures past.
With nimble fingers, they spin and twine,
In patterns of fate, so bold, divine.

Dreams blossom softly, like night-blooming flowers,
In the woodlands' embrace during midnight hours.
With magic untold, they drift and sway,
Enchanting our minds, come what may.

In the quiet hush of twilight's glow,
The dreamweavers come, their magic flows.
Through whispered dreams, our hearts they grace,
In the sacred space, we find our place.

The Lullaby of Muffled Light and Leaf

In twilight's hush, a lullaby sings,
Of muffled light and the peace it brings.
The whispers of leaves in soft embrace,
Cradle the world in a gentle space.

The stars they blink through branches tight,
As crickets chirp their serenade bright.
Each note a promise of sweet repose,
In nature's arms, where love bestows.

With every sigh of the evening breeze,
The heart finds solace beneath the trees.
A lull of peace in the growing dark,
Where dreams take flight, igniting a spark.

So close your eyes, let worries fade,
Embrace the calm that the night has laid.
In muffled light, let your spirit soar,
To the lullaby of the woods' soft lore.

Secrets of the Faery Glen

In the glen where shadows play,
Whispers of the night do sway.
Hidden paths of emerald hue,
Secrets old, known to but few.

Pixies dance on dewy leaves,
Spinning tales that hearts believe.
Moonlight bathes the world in dreams,
Where the faery laughter gleams.

Winding streams of silver bright,
Carrying wishes into the night.
Here, the ancient magic flows,
In every breeze, a story grows.

Cloaked in mist, the willows sigh,
As time drifts like clouds on high.
In the glen, where spirits dwell,
Adventure waits, a timeless spell.

So heed the call of softest sound,
In Faery Glen, enchantments abound.
With every step, let wonder rise,
As secrets stir beneath the skies.

Misty Echoes from the Hollow

In the hollow, shadows weave,
Misty echoes give and leave.
Whispers dance on twilight air,
Secrets known, yet none would dare.

Glimmers flicker in the dark,
Fireflies light the way, a spark.
Each breath holds tales of yore,
Misty dreams that linger more.

The ancient trees, their branches bow,
Guarding treasures of the now.
In each rustle, stories bloom,
As whispers break the silent gloom.

Nighttime weaves a silken thread,
Binding hearts where dreams are led.
Echoes soft like lullabies,
Awake the magic, hush the ties.

So journey forth, let spirits guide,
Through misty paths where secrets hide.
In the hollow, magic flows,
Embrace the night, let wonder grow.

Delicate Tapestry of Starlight

Beyond the veil of dusk's embrace,
Lies a tapestry of grace.
Threaded with each starry gleam,
Weaving softly through a dream.

Galaxies twirl in velvet skies,
Whispers of the night arise.
Constellations softly sway,
Guiding wanderers on their way.

The moon, a guardian above,
Watches with the hand of love.
In the stillness, dreams take flight,
In delicate waltzes of the night.

Each twinkle tells a tale anew,
Of hidden paths and skies so blue.
So take a moment, breathe it in,
Feel the magic deep within.

For in this tapestry of light,
Each stitch is woven with delight.
A dance, a spark, a fleeting trace,
In the starlight's warm embrace.

Charmed Whirls of the Elfin Breeze

In the realms where elfin whispers sigh,
Charmed whirls swirl and gently fly.
On fragrant winds, the secrets drift,
As nature's heart begins to lift.

A dance of leaves in golden glow,
Where every breeze brings tales to know.
In every breath, enchantments tease,
With hints of magic in the breeze.

Through arching trees, the pathways gleam,
Casting visions like a dream.
Elfin laughter, light and free,
Fills the air with melody.

Connection deep, a timeless thread,
Binding spirits where love is bred.
Feel the pulse of earth so near,
In the dance of the breezes clear.

So let your heart embrace the muse,
In charming whirls, it's yours to choose.
With every flutter, every sound,
In elfin ease, adventure's found.

Whispers of Gossamer Dreams

In the hush of night, whispers glide,
Through silvered woods where secrets hide.
Starlit paths twine softly bright,
Guided by moon, a lantern's light.

Dreams woven fine in silken threads,
Where wishes dance on feathered beds.
Magic hums in shadows' embrace,
Gossamer wings in velvet space.

A breeze carries tales of yore,
To the shores of the dreamer's door.
With every sigh, the heart may take,
A leap of faith, a wish to make.

Laughter echoes, soft and sweet,
In twilight's realm, where shadows meet.
With each heartbeat, a soft refrain,
In the realm where hope remains.

Shadows of Moonlit Faeries

Beneath the silver moon's soft glow,
Faeries flit, a shimmering show.
With laughter light as the morning dew,
They weave their paths where dreams come true.

In glades where secrets quietly bloom,
The night is wrapped in sweet perfume.
They whisper tales of love and cheer,
To hearts that listen, so sincere.

Wands of light in hands so small,
They conjure wishes, one and all.
With dances spun in twilight air,
They paint the dark with magic rare.

Shadows flit 'neath the ancient trees,
Carried forth on a gentle breeze.
In moonlit nights, their spirits call,
A timeless song that binds us all.

Enchanted Threads of Twilight

Threads of twilight weave through the dusk,
In colors rich, like velvet husk.
With every stitch, the night takes flight,
In magic's cloak, all hearts ignite.

Whispers linger in the twilight's loom,
Where the stars emerge from the gloom.
A tapestry of dreams unfolds,
In hues of silver, stories told.

Crickets chirp their soft sweet song,
To the dance of shadows, all belong.
As darkness falls and spirits rise,
The fabric glimmers, under skies.

In ancient woods where wishes call,
Lay enchanted threads that bind us all.
With every breath, the night conceives,
A world where magic never leaves.

Soft Lullabies of the Forest

In the heart of woods, where silence hums,
Soft lullabies of nature comes.
The breeze sings low through branches high,
A gentle call, a sweet goodbye.

Mossy beds, where shadows lie,
Kissed by dew, as daylight sighs.
A squirrel scampers, a songbird trills,
In harmony, the forest fills.

With whispers sweet, the night unfolds,
In stories woven, endlessly told.
A cradle of peace, where dreams take wing,
In the heart of night, the forest sings.

Stars watch over with twinkling eyes,
Guardians of lullabies in the skies.
Rest, dear heart, the world awaits,
Where magic lives at nature's gates.

A Tapestry of Fae Folklore

In glades where whispers softly tread,
The gentle fae weave dreams of light.
With gossamer wings and laughter spread,
They dance in shadows kissed by night.

A golden thread of tales untold,
Each stitch a secret, rich and rare.
In moonlit whispers, brave and bold,
They spin their magic through the air.

With every flicker, hope ignites,
A tapestry of wishes spun.
In evening's glow, beginnings bright,
Adventure's song has just begun.

From elder trees and bubbling brooks,
They gather echoes of the past.
Each smile a story, like well-read books,
Their legacy forever cast.

So wander where the wild things are,
And listen to the music near.
For in the glow of every star,
The fae's enchantment becomes clear.

Elusive Glimmers in the Night's Grasp

In twilight's cloak, the secrets hide,
Elusive glimmers tease the eye.
With fleeting grace, the shadows glide,
Inviting whispers from the sky.

Beneath the moon's enchanted gaze,
Shimmers dance on currents weaved.
In hidden paths where dreams amaze,
The heart finds solace, warmly grieved.

A crackling fire, its embers sing,
While owls converse in wise decree.
The night unfolds its darkened wing,
Revealing worlds both wild and free.

Though mystic fog may veil the way,
In stillness, magic breathes and plays.
Each flicker, hint of what may stay,
For dawn will cradle night's soft rays.

So let your heart embrace the night,
With every glimmer, feel the spark.
For in the dark, there hides delight,
A world alive, a glowing arc.

Shadows Beneath the Canopy of Stars

Beneath the spread of starlit skies,
The shadows weave their ancient tale.
Where dreams and wonders softly rise,
In every sigh, the stories sail.

The whispering leaves, a gentle choir,
Sing songs of ages lost in time.
With every breath, the world aspires,
To find the rhythm, pure and sublime.

In tangled roots and hidden trails,
The heartbeat of the earth resounds.
Through moonlit glades where magic prevails,
Life dances softly, joy unbound.

With echoes of a past long gone,
The shadows beckon, secrets found.
So lose yourself until the dawn,
In this enchanted, mystic ground.

As stars above ignite the bay,
Let ancient whispers guide your way.
For in the night, the heart will sway,
With every shadow, dreams shall play.

Luminous Wonders of Enchanted Evenings

In evenings brushed with softest light,
Luminous wonders fill the air.
With every twinkle, hearts take flight,
In stillness found, the magic's rare.

The meadows glow with phantom grace,
As fireflies weave a tapestry.
Each flicker dances, sweet embrace,
In whispered dreams of what can be.

Through winding paths and quiet streams,
The night unveils its jeweled crown.
With every shadow, hope redeems,
The canvas bright, a rare renown.

So gather close, the stories share,
In circles formed with friends so true.
For every heart laid gently bare,
Will find its kin beneath the blue.

As morning glimmers on the rise,
Embrace the echoes of the night.
For in those fleeting, starry skies,
Lies every soul's illuminating light.

Secrets of the Wanderers in the Wood

In the hush of the twilight's weave,
Whispers dance where shadows cleave.
Footsteps light on mossy ground,
Secrets linger, softly bound.

Branches sway with ancient grace,
Echoes of a hidden place.
Moonlit paths, where wild things roam,
Hearts entwined to nature's foam.

Rustling leaves, a fleeting glance,
Mysteries in a wild romance.
Beyond the veil of daily strife,
Magic brews, infusing life.

In the ink of night so deep,
Guardians of the woods will keep.
Chasing dreams on starlit trails,
In their eyes, the lost tales sail.

Dance, oh spirit, twirl and glide,
Through the woods where wonders hide.
In the realm of sylvan dreams,
Every shadow softly gleams.

Gentle Spirals of Nature's Breath

Windswept meadows, secret flowers,
Nature's breath in fleeting hours.
Spirals twirl in soft refrain,
Caressing earth with sweet, sweet rain.

Rippling streams and rustling grass,
Time ebbs gently, moments pass.
Every leaf a whispered song,
In the dance where we belong.

The sun dips low, the shadows grow,
In amber light, the soft winds blow.
Egrets soar on skyward wings,
Nature's heart, it beats and sings.

Each breath taken, each sigh released,
In nature's arms, our souls are eased.
We spiral gently, heart anew,
In her embrace, our spirits true.

With every dusk, a promise made,
In twilight's glow, no love will fade.
Gentle whispers in the air,
Nature's breath, a sacred prayer.

Soft Echoes Carrying Tales Untold

In the quiet of the glade,
Soft echoes of the past cascades.
Through twisted roots, stories roam,
Carrying whispers of their home.

Winds of change, a subtle guide,
Let the heart and soul collide.
With every shadow, every light,
Tales unfurl, the day and night.

Stars above, like secrets shared,
In the depths, a world prepared.
Echoes of laughter, tears once shed,
In every word, the journey spread.

Listen closely to the sighs,
In the hush where the spirit flies.
A tapestry of dreams entwined,
Soft echoes weave the ties that bind.

Timeless stories, old and wise,
In the hush where the nightbird cries.
Carry them forth, let them unfold,
Soft echoes bright, tales untold.

Faery Lights on the Winds of Change

Cotton clouds in twilight's glow,
Whispers sing where faery winds blow.
Softly glimmers of light abound,
A dance of fate in circles round.

Flickering flames in the dusky air,
Guided past the dreams we share.
Chasing shadows, hearts in flight,
Faery lights ignite the night.

Through the valleys, where wishes bloom,
Ethereal voices break the gloom.
Upon the breeze, let worries wane,
Embrace the magic, feel no pain.

Sweet revelations born from chance,
Life's unfolding, a spirited dance.
With every turn, let hope arrange,
The faery lights on winds of change.

As dawn approaches, softly glow,
The mysteries of the day will flow.
Find your path on golden rays,
In faery lights, your spirit stays.

Moonlit Riddles of the Fey

In the glade where shadows dance,
Moonlit whispers hold a chance.
Fey folk gather, laughter bright,
Weaving dreams in silver light.

Secrets hidden in the trees,
A breeze carries ancient pleas.
Mysteries twine, like vines around,
With every riddle, magic's found.

Stars above, a watchful guide,
Winking down with spark and pride.
Elven voices, soft as sighs,
Chant through night, where silence flies.

Glimmers spark on dew-kissed leaves,
Where each heart has strength to weave.
In this realm of whispered fate,
Dancing steps seal every date.

So tread carefully, dreamer bold,
In this land of tales retold.
For every riddle, treasure's near,
In laughter shared, in joy sincere.

Serene Pathways of Gentle Light

Beneath the boughs of willow trees,
Softly drift the evening breeze.
Luminous paths, so calm and bright,
Guide lost souls with tender light.

Each footstep whispers tales untold,
Of wandering hearts and dreams of gold.
Through soft glades where shadows play,
Serenity leads the way.

Crickets sing in dusk's embrace,
Time slows down at nature's pace.
Moonbeams dance on rippling streams,
Cradling softly all our dreams.

Echoes of laughter from the past,
In memory's grip, forever cast.
Dance along this tranquil shore,
Where peace resides forevermore.

So walk this path with gentle grace,
And discover your sacred place.
For in each step, a world ignites,
In serene pathways of gentle light.

Mystical Threads of the Twilight Realm

As day gives way to night's embrace,
In twilight's breath, find your space.
Threads of magic intertwine,
Binding realms where dreams align.

Stars awaken with a shimmer,
Illuminating shadows dimmer.
Woven tales in colors bright,
Cast a glow, enchanting sight.

Mystical realms, where wishes fly,
In every glance, a wonder sigh.
A tapestry of fate unfolds,
Whispers shared, and courage bold.

Dance with shadows, brave and free,
In the twilight, find the key.
Unlock the mysteries of the night,
For every heart possesses light.

So weave your dreams, let them soar,
In these threads, forevermore.
Mystical journeys ever swell,
In twilight's veil, we weave our spell.

Ethereal Murmurs Beneath the Stars

Whispers float on midnight air,
Ethereal murmurs everywhere.
Each star a story, softly told,
Of wandering hearts, so brave and bold.

Curious dreams upon the breeze,
Stirring gently through the trees.
Listen close, for secrets sigh,
Beneath the vast, embracing sky.

Night unveils its velvet veil,
As moonbeams glimmer, bright and pale.
In every heartbeat, magic flows,
A symphony that softly glows.

In the stillness, time stands still,
Every moment, a dream to fulfill.
With every twinkle, every glance,
The universe calls you to dance.

So gather close, let stardust drift,
In sacred space, feel the gift.
With ethereal murmurs in the air,
Find your peace, find your care.

Songs of the Serene Sylphs

In twilight's hush, where shadows dwell,
Whispers float like a gentle spell.
Sylphs in dance, with grace they glide,
Beneath the moon, their secrets bide.

With laughter bright, they weave the air,
Threads of magic, light as prayer.
A flicker here, a shimmer there,
Songs of wonder, beyond compare.

Through leafy canopies, they play,
Chasing dreams that drift away.
Jubilant hearts in sparkling throng,
In a symphony, they belong.

From dew-kissed blooms, their voices rise,
A melody that never dies.
In harmony with night's embrace,
Sylphs enchant this sacred space.

So listen close, beneath the stars,
The songs of sylphs, near and far.
In every breeze, their laughter lies,
A serenade to silent skies.

Breeze-carried Hints of Fairy Feasts

Among the roots of ancient trees,
Fairies gather on the breeze.
With tiny cups of nectar sweet,
They share their joys, their hearts' heartbeat.

Twinkling lights in shadows play,
Marking night from fading day.
Gathered round with merry song,
A feast so bright, the brave belong.

Petals soft, like silken cloth,
Spread beneath, they dance and froth.
Mirthful laughter fills the air,
Hints of feasts in moonlit flare.

Glimmers of gold, a treasure rare,
On mushroom tops, the finest fare.
With every nibble, every sip,
Joyful hearts begin to flip.

So on the wind, like whispers sweet,
Find fairy feasts where shadows meet.
A wondrous night in nature's thrall,
Breeze that carries hints of all.

Delicate Secrets of Nature's Palette

In gardens lush, where colors bloom,
Nature paints with fragrant plume.
Delicate secrets, softly spun,
In every petal, a story begun.

Hues of violet, whispers of rose,
Each shade a tale that gently flows.
Sunlight dapples through the trees,
Nature's palette, a tapestry with ease.

With every dawn, a fresh embrace,
Brush strokes of light, a tender grace.
Golden rays on morning dew,
Nature whispers, soft and true.

In twilight's glow, the colors blend,
An artist's hand that cannot end.
Through seasons' change, the hues repeat,
Secrets held, both warm and sweet.

So roam the fields, the meadows wide,
With open hearts and arms spread wide.
In every bloom, let beauty be,
Delicate secrets, wild and free.

Enchanted Gleams of the Wood Nymphs

In forests deep, where echoes dwell,
Wood nymphs weave their magic spell.
With laughter light, they flit and float,
On whispers soft, like dreams they wrote.

Emerald glades and silver streams,
Hold the essence of ancient dreams.
With every step, a symphony,
As nymphs dance wild and free.

In shadowed glens, where secrets sigh,
They weave the words of earth and sky.
Gentle breezes, soft and sweet,
Carry nymphs on silvered feet.

With glimmers bright, they light the night,
Stars above that twinkle bright.
In moonlit glamor, they unite,
Enchanting all within their sight.

So wander forth in woodlands fair,
And with the nymphs, your dreams declare.
In every rustle, every gleam,
Find the magic of a dream.

Whirls of Season's Secrets

In autumn's breath, the leaves do sway,
Whispers of secrets, in twilight's play.
A dance of colors, bold and bright,
Nature unfurls her joyful sight.

Winter's hush, a blanket white,
Crystals glisten, in soft moonlight.
Silent stories the stars have spun,
In quiet dreams, the year is done.

Springtime stirs with gentle hands,
Awakens life in sunlit lands.
Blossoms burst forth, a fragrant cheer,
Hope and joy each day draws near.

Summer's warmth, a golden hue,
With laughter echoing in skies so blue.
Adventure beckons from each warm breeze,
Dancing shadows beneath the trees.

A cycle weaves, in time's embrace,
Nature's canvas, a wondrous space.
In each season, life's secrets bide,
A tapestry where dreams reside.

Tides of Time in Sylvan Glimmers

In shadowed groves where whispers sigh,
Moonlit beams through branches fly.
The forest breathes, in peace it dwells,
Stirring tales that nature tells.

Time drifts gently like roots that weave,
Through hidden paths, in webs we believe.
Echoes linger in the night air,
Elfin laughter, a sweet, soft prayer.

Rippling streams, they gleam and flow,
Carrying secrets only they know.
Through sylvan glades, the wonders gleam,
In every glance, a whispered dream.

Beneath the stars, the world spins slow,
Each moment cherished in evening's glow.
The tides of time, they ebb and flow,
In nature's heart, we find our glow.

Winding paths of memories made,
In woodland realms, our fears allayed.
While echoes murmur of long ago,
In sylvan glimmers, our spirits grow.

Echoes of the Elfin Dreamscape

Beneath the boughs where shadows creep,
An elfin world begins to leap.
In twilight's hush, the magic hums,
With every breath, the dreamscape drums.

Misty veils and whispering trees,
Carried softly on the breeze.
Glimmers of starlight dance and play,
Guiding lost souls who stray away.

A symphony of night unfolds,
In shimmering tales of old retold.
With silvered streams and moonlit skies,
The echoes sing a sweet reprise.

Hold fast your dreams, let them take flight,
On wings of wonder, through the night.
For in each heart, a spark resides,
A glimpse of magic that abides.

So let us roam in twilight's grace,
Through the elfin dreamscape, we embrace.
In every whisper, every sigh,
The echoes promise, dreams never die.

Gentle Flutters of Nature's Secrets

In morning mist, where shadows lay,
Gentle flutters lead the way.
Butterflies dance among the blooms,
In nature's heart, a song consumes.

Soft whispers of the lapping streams,
Carry the weight of hidden dreams.
Petals fall like whispered sighs,
Nature's secrets, soft and shy.

Beneath the boughs, the wild things play,
In the dappled light of the day.
The rustling leaves, a soft refrain,
A melody sweet like summer rain.

As twilight glows, the world unspools,
Spilling secrets of ancient pools.
Frogs croak softly, crickets sing,
In this embrace, magic takes wing.

Nature unveils her tender might,
Framing dreams in silver light.
In every flutter, every sigh,
Nature's secrets never die.

Whimsy Woven in Enchanted Realms

In a glade where fairies play,
Colors twist and dreams ballet.
Laughter lifts on breezy wings,
As twilight softly hums and sings.

Beneath the boughs of ancient trees,
Magic drips like honeyed bees.
Whispers echo through the night,
In realms where shadows spark delight.

With every twirl, a story spun,
Of lost spells and races run.
Time unravels, threads unwind,
In the heart where wonders bind.

A potion brewed with starlit tea,
A crown of flowers, wild and free.
Chasing dreams through dappled light,
In enchanted realms of pure delight.

So when you wander, close your eyes,
Listen for the secret sighs.
In whimsy's weave, let spirits play,
And find your magic every day.

Shadows Danced in the Moonbeams

Amidst the night, where shadows swirl,
Moonbeams flicker, secrets unfurl.
In silver light, the gentle sway,
Of whispers wrapped in twilight's gray.

Figures dart with playful grace,
In darkened corners, they leave a trace.
Each flicker sparks a tale to tell,
Of ancient woods where spirits dwell.

The owls gaze down with knowing eyes,
While magic twirls across the skies.
As shadows dance, the night takes flight,
And dreams entwine with silver light.

Through tangled trees and misty veils,
The tunes of night weave secret tales.
In every pause, a heartbeat thumps,
In shadow's embrace, the world just jumps.

So walk with me where the wild things play,
In moonlit realms where shadows sway.
With every step, our laughter blends,
In the dance where the magic never ends.

Celestial Threads of the Mystic Sky

Stars embroider the night so deep,
In velvet skies where dreamers sleep.
Galaxies spin like dervishes bright,
Woven threads of cosmic light.

Each constellation tells a tale,
Of sailors, lovers, and ships that sail.
The moon, a guardian on her throne,
Guides lost souls, so far from home.

Through celestial tides, we drift along,
In a chorus of a timeless song.
Comets blaze, and heavens sing,
In the tapestry that the cosmos brings.

A dance of fate in stellar flight,
Each twirling star, a wish ignites.
So look above and find your place,
In the endless beauty of time and space.

Embrace the threads that bind us all,
In the mystic sky, we hear the call.
Together we weave a radiant thread,
In the dreamscape where the stars are fed.

Elfin Passages through Silken Mists

In realms where elfin whispers float,
Through silken mists, a fleeting boat.
They glide on paths of gentle dew,
Where ancient secrets beckon you.

In twilight's breath, the shadows play,
While moonbeams guide the lost astray.
Through haunted woods and crystal streams,
A world unfolds of fleeting dreams.

With every step, the echoes sigh,
In love with life, we wander by.
The leaves, like laughter, softly rustle,
In elfin hearts, we find our bustle.

Among the ferns and whispering trees,
A hidden realm where time's a breeze.
As soft light dances on the air,
Magic glistens everywhere.

So seek the paths that twist and turn,
In silken mists, let your heart yearn.
For in the glades, we come alive,
In elfin joys, our dreams will thrive.

Celestial Wands in the Forest's Heart

In shadows deep where secrets lie,
The wands of light begin to fly.
A whisper weaves through ancient trees,
As spirits dance upon the breeze.

With fingers wrapped in twilight's glow,
They summon stars from woods below.
A gentle pulse in earth and vine,
The forest breathes, its magic divine.

Beneath a canopy of dreams,
What once was lost, now brightly gleams.
Each wand a tale, a heartbeat's thread,
In every flicker, magic's spread.

And softly hums the sylvan song,
Where weary souls can learn to belong.
Drawn by the light, they start to sway,
Amidst the trees, they'll find their way.

With every footfall, blooms anew,
The forest glows, in vibrant hue.
Celestial wands take flight tonight,
In nature's embrace, pure and bright.

The Trance of Starlit Wanderings

Under a canvas of midnight blue,
The stars awaken, a shimmering view.
A path appears, paved with light,
Guiding hearts through the silent night.

In whispered songs the shadows drift,
As dreams and wishes gently lift.
The moon, a guardian, watches near,
Embracing all who wander here.

With every step upon the glade,
The starlit trance begins to fade.
And yet, in stillness, memories weave,
A tapestry of hope we cleave.

Among the trees, the echoes play,
A waltz of stars that lights the way.
Each wanderer finds their heart's refrain,
In the mystic hush, they'll sing again.

So follow where the night winds call,
Let starlit dreams embrace you all.
For in the dance of shifting light,
A world awakens, pure delight.

Enchantment Within the Hushed Mornings

In the dawn's embrace, soft and warm,
Awakens nature, a tranquil charm.
With dew-kissed blooms, life starts anew,
A symphony, the sky's fresh hue.

Each ray of sun, a golden note,
The world arises, a gentle coat.
Within the hush, the spirits sigh,
As whispers of magic fill the sky.

With every breath, the heart expands,
In morning's light, where enchantment stands.
A spell is cast on roots and leaves,
In silent moments, the forest breathes.

With open eyes, the wonders bloom,
A canvas bright, dispelling gloom.
For beauty lies where silence dwells,
In every nook, the magic swells.

So wander softly, tread with grace,
For in the morn, you'll find your place.
Embrace the light, the soft refrain,
In the stillness, find love's sweet gain.

Stardust Trails Amidst Woodland Spells

Above the trees where shadows play,
Stardust trails lead lovers astray.
With twinkling eyes, they follow forth,
In search of magic, joy, and worth.

Each step unveils a whispered dream,
A woodland path, a silvery gleam.
With every heartbeat, secrets shared,
In twilit glades, a journey bared.

The trees entwined, they seem to sway,
In harmony, both night and day.
A sprinkle of hope, a touch of grace,
Within the woods, a sacred space.

With every rustle, every sigh,
The stars above begin to cry.
For in their shimmering, ancient lore,
The woodland spells forever soar.

So wander on, let stardust guide,
Through realms where secret worlds abide.
For in the heart of hidden trails,
Lie wondrous tales where magic prevails.

Threads of Laughter Under Silver Leaves

In twilight hours when shadows dance,
The whispers weave a playful trance.
Beneath the boughs of ancient trees,
The laughter twirls upon the breeze.

Glimmers of joy in every glance,
With silver leaves they start to prance.
The world unfolds a secret scheme,
Where every night can spark a dream.

Echoes of friends who've come and gone,
They sing their tales as stars looked on.
In the soft glow, their joy survives,
In threads of laughter, magic thrives.

A winding path through dusk's embrace,
Where playful spirits find their place.
With every step, a heart grows bold,
In silver leaves, pure joy unfolds.

As night descends, the world seems bright,
In harmony, they take their flight.
For in the grove, with laughter's grace,
Their woven joy, time can't erase.

The Enigma of Roving Spirits

Beneath the moon, the shadows glide,
In stillness where the secrets hide.
A flicker here, a whisper there,
The roaming spirits fill the air.

They dance on winds of ancient tales,
With laughter echoing in the gales.
Through misty paths, they weave their way,
In twilight's cloak, they love to play.

Curious eyes in emerald hues,
They gather dreams like morning dew.
Each fleeting glance unfolds a truth,
In gentle hearts, they guard our youth.

With every breath, the night azure,
The mysteries swell and they allure.
In harmony, they glide and drift,
The roving spirits, nature's gift.

They slip through branches, soft and light,
Creating wonders in the night.
Entwining souls with whispers low,
The enigma of life they sow.

Dappled Light and Hidden Laughter

In glades where sunlight spills and twirls,
The magic plays in gentle whirls.
Dappled light on mossy floor,
Unfolds the joys we can explore.

Beneath the canopy so wide,
With every step, the heart's our guide.
Hidden laughter rings like bells,
In secret nooks where friendship dwells.

The rustle of leaves that softly sigh,
Calls forth the dreams that wander by.
With every shade and glimmer bright,
The forest sings, delighting sight.

Through winding paths where wonders thrive,
The joys of youth will stay alive.
In whispers shared, the bonds grow tight,
In dappled light, there's pure delight.

As day departs and night draws near,
The laughter lingers, sweet and clear.
For in this grove, with every glance,
Dappled light sparks our hearts to dance.

Secrets of the Grove's Gentle Keepers

In sacred woods where shadows rest,
The gentle keepers weave their best.
With whispers soft, they guard the lore,
In every heart, a secret door.

They tend the blooms with loving care,
Beneath the moon's enchanted stare.
In twilight hours, they share their sights,
Where dreams take flight on starlit nights.

With every rustling leaf above,
They call to us with tender love.
Through winding trails of cool embrace,
The grove unveils its hidden grace.

Moments cherished, memories spun,
The gentle keepers' work is done.
With joyful hearts, the stories flow,
In every breath, their magic grows.

As dawn awakens with a sigh,
The keepers vanish, yet they nigh.
In every tree, their essence stays,
Guardians of dreams in sunlit rays.

Gentle Swirls of Forgotten Lore

In shadows soft where secrets dwell,
The faded tales begin to swell.
With every whisper of the breeze,
Old stories dance among the trees.

Each leaf a page, each twig a word,
In the quiet, ancient songs are heard.
A tapestry of time unwinds,
Weaving dreams of lost designs.

The brook will sing of yesteryears,
Of laughter, joy, and gentle tears.
In twilight's grasp, the past shines bright,
A fleeting glimpse of purest light.

Here, wise owls perch on weary boughs,
Guardians of the night's soft vows.
They hoot of love and battles fought,
In every echo, wisdom sought.

Mist curls like smoke upon the ground,
Where every path has stories found.
The moonlit glimmer, soft and slow,
Guides wanderers where lore will flow.

Dreams Entwined in Selkie's Embrace

Beneath the waves where shadows play,
The selkie dreams by night and day.
Her skin of seal, her heart of song,
In ocean's depths, she swims along.

Moonlight dances on the tide,
Where secrets of the deep abide.
A silver glint in water's heart,
Each ripple forms a work of art.

She weaves her dreams with silky trails,
And whispers soft of ancient gales.
A melody that calls the brave,
To uncharted realms beneath the wave.

With every sunset, sorrows fade,
As starlit paths through waters wade.
Her laughter like a gentle wave,
Embraces souls, the lost and brave.

In twilight's hush, she breathes the air,
A fleeting glimpse, a heartfelt stare.
Come, listen close, her tale unfolds,
In woven dreams, the heart consoled.

Echoes of the Fabletellers

By fireside glow, the fabletellers,
Spin ancient yarns like wondrous dwellers.
With every word, the room ignites,
Filling hearts with magic sights.

In every shadow, characters loom,
Heroes rise from the dusk's soft gloom.
Their laughter echoes through the night,
A tapestry of pure delight.

The tales of yore, of love and loss,
Resound with joy, no matter the cost.
In whispered tones, they hide and seek,
The souls of all who dared to speak.

From distant lands where legends thrive,
The spirits of the brave arrive.
As twilight deepens, dreams take flight,
The fabletellers weave the night.

So gather close, let stories weave,
In every heart, the tales believe.
For through the magic, we shall find,
A world where wonder leaves us blind.

Nectar-laden Whispers of Twilight

In the garden where the shadows creep,
The whispers dance and secrets sleep.
With petals wet from evening dew,
The twilight sings a lullaby true.

Each breeze a note, each flower a song,
In fragrant air, the night belongs.
Nectar-laden, the blossoms sway,
Inviting the stars to join the play.

The crickets chirp a rhythmic call,
A symphony to cradle all.
As fireflies twinkle, softly bright,
Painting dreams across the night.

In this haven, worries cease,
A tapestry of gentle peace.
With every breath, the world unfolds,
A whispered promise in twilight holds.

So linger here, let time stand still,
In nectar-rich air, feel the thrill.
For in this dusk, we find our place,
A moment caught in sweet embrace.

Seraphic Murmurs in Dappled Groves

Beneath the boughs where whispers play,
The light of dreams begins to stray.
Wings of the angels softly hum,
In the dappled shade where shadows come.

Petals blush with the morning light,
Each flutter whispers secrets bright.
Nature's grace in every sigh,
As time slips gently, passing by.

Amidst the ferns and ancient trees,
A melody carried by the breeze.
In twilight's glow, the magic swells,
With every note, a story dwells.

Seraphic murmurs weave the air,
In this enchanted world so rare.
The heart finds solace, pure and sweet,
In echoes of the forest's beat.

Let dreams take root within this place,
Where sunlight dances, leaves embrace.
With every breath, a bond we make,
In dappled groves, our spirits wake.

Twilight's Embrace in the Wonderland

In twilight's arms, the world transforms,
As gentle whispers fill the norms.
The colors blend, a sweet surprise,
In the wonderland where magic lies.

Moonbeams play on dewy grass,
Awakening dreams that softly pass.
A trail of starlight beckons near,
Creating paths where none appear.

Frogs croak secrets by the stream,
As shadows dance in a twinkling dream.
The fireflies weave a glowing thread,
Guiding those who've softly fled.

The night's embrace, both calm and deep,
Holds the mysteries we long to keep.
With every pulse, a story spins,
As twilight's magic softly begins.

In this space where wonders meet,
Hope arises, warm and sweet.
Let us linger, let us play,
In twilight's arms, we drift away.

Glimmers of Hope in Twilight's Reach

When shadows stretch and dusk appears,
A quiet hush replaces fears.
Glimmers of hope dance in the skies,
Illuminating dreams that rise.

In every corner, secrets dwell,
With tales of joy that hearts can tell.
The nightingale sings its soothing song,
Where the lost and weary belong.

Stars awaken with a gentle glow,
Kindling the dreams we cherish so.
Each flicker whispers, 'Do not roam,'
For in this twilight, we find home.

Through velvet skies and silver streams,
We gather strength from whispered dreams.
With every breath, the magic grows,
In twilight's reach, our spirit flows.

So let the night bring peace anew,
As hope ignites in skies so blue.
With stars to guide, we will ignite,
The flames of love in the deep twilight.

Enigmatic Wonders Beneath Ancient Boughs

Beneath ancient boughs, where secrets lay,
Enigmatic wonders come out to play.
Riddles echo through the hazy air,
Inviting those who wander there.

Leaves rustle softly, a subtle sigh,
Revealing truths as the moments fly.
The forest breathes in whispered tones,
Where every shadow hides its own.

Crimson berries, glistening bright,
Hold magic wrapped in the dying light.
Underneath the ferns, a spark takes flight,
Igniting wonder in the heart of night.

Every branch a story, every root a tale,
In the dwelling place where dreams set sail.
With every step, adventure blooms,
Where nature's heart forever looms.

So listen closely, and you may find,
The wisdom waiting for the kind.
Enigmatic wonders, a gentle tease,
Beneath the boughs, where hearts find ease.

Dreams Weaved with Dew-kissed Petals

In twilight's grasp, where magic stirs,
A tapestry of whispers furrows,
Beneath the stars, soft dreams unfurl,
On petals kissed by morning's pearls.

Fluttered thoughts in dreams' embrace,
With silver beams and moonlight's trace,
A dance of hope on fragrant air,
In nature's arms, we weave our care.

The world adorned with dreams galore,
Each drop a tale, a secret lore,
A garden rich with colors bright,
Awakens hearts, ignites the night.

With gentle hands, we breathe anew,
In every petal, life rings true,
We chase the dawn, let shadows flee,
In dew's soft touch, we find the key.

So let us wander, hand in hand,
Through fields of dreams, in magic land,
Where dew-kissed petals guide our way,
And dance with dreams till break of day.

The Dance of Elfin Shadows

In moonlight's glow, the shadows play,
Elfin pirouettes, a soft ballet,
Through whispering woods, they weave and sway,
Dancing in twilight's gentle spray.

A hidden path where secrets dwell,
With laughter echoing like a spell,
Through brimming leaves and silver streams,
They twirl like wisps of dreaming beams.

The night unfurls its velvet sheet,
As elfin feet, on silence, greet,
With every turn, the air ignites,
In harmony, with starry lights.

Their laughter mingles, light and free,
A tapestry of fantasy,
In every swirl, in every glance,
They weave a tapestry of chance.

So linger here, as shadows blend,
With elfin grace that knows no end,
In every heart, their magic lives,
A dance eternal that love gives.

Enchantment in the Hollow's Heart

In hidden glades, where silence meets,
The hollow's heart, where magic beats,
A whisper sings of ancient lore,
In secrets held forevermore.

With mossy carpets, soft and deep,
Where time stands still, and shadows creep,
The dance of leaves, the breeze's sigh,
In dreamlike realms, we learn to fly.

A flicker bright, a firefly's glow,
Guides wandering souls through twilight's flow,
In every breath, in every sigh,
The hollow hums, a lullaby.

With tender care, embrace the night,
In starlit paths, find pure delight,
For in this place, where spirits dwell,
An enchantment spun, a timeless spell.

So hold your dreams, and let them soar,
In hollowed hearts, we seek for more,
With every step, let wonder start,
In the enchanting hollow's heart.

Glistening Meanders of Lost Magics

Through silver streams, where secrets flow,
Glistening meanders, charms aglow,
In currents deep, the spirits twine,
In whispered tales, their fates entwine.

The banks adorned in emerald hues,
With breezes soft, and morning dews,
Each ripple sings of long-lost days,
Of magic spun in countless ways.

In twilight's grasp, where dreams convene,
The echoes of a world once seen,
Each bend a portal, each turn a clue,
To magic lost, but still held true.

So seek the paths where wildflowers play,
In meandering trails, where fairies sway,
For in each drop, a story lies,
A glistening glimpse of endless skies.

Embrace the journey, heed the call,
In endless wonder, let your spirit sprawl,
For glistening meanders safely guide,
The seeker's heart, where lost magics abide.

Ethereal Dances Amongst the Foliage

In the glade where shadows play,
Whispers flutter like a sway.
Leaves alive, they twist and twirl,
Nature's dream in a gentle swirl.

Moonlight filters through the green,
Casting spells in the unseen.
Twinkling stars begin to glance,
Land of magic, a midnight dance.

Fairies flit with laughter bright,
Filling the air with sheer delight.
Petals shimmer with grace untold,
Tales of wonder begin to unfold.

The night draws close with a shush,
Each sound wrapped in a quiet hush.
Dancing leaves under silver skies,
Echo the secret of ancient cries.

Yet when dawn begins to break,
Fleeting dreams, the world will take.
But in the heart where memory stirs,
The ethereal dance forever whirs.

Secret Song of the Starlit Grove

In the grove where shadows sing,
Moonbeams weave a silver ring.
Stars above, like diamonds bright,
Sing of magic, love, and light.

Whispers rise on gentle air,
Stories dwell in secrets rare.
Nature's hymn, both soft and low,
Invites the heart to gently flow.

Crickets chirp a lullaby,
Beneath a vast and wondrous sky.
Each note dances on the breeze,
Bringing forth a sense of ease.

Within the wood, the shadows play,
Leading the night with soft ballet.
Branches sway in time with dreams,
Carving paths of silken beams.

As the world begins to fade,
Fueling the creeks where magic's laid.
The secret song will always bloom,
In hearts where wildflowers loom.

Misty Echoes of Faery Delights

In the mist where fairies roam,
Whispers carry tales back home.
Glimmers of laughter, soft and light,
Guide the heart through endless night.

Beneath the boughs of ancient trees,
Echoes travel on the breeze.
Sprinkling dreams of wonder deep,
In every shadow, secrets sleep.

Guided by the moon's embrace,
Time stands still in this sacred place.
Dearest wishes softly spoken,
Misty echoes, bonds unbroken.

Where wildflowers bloom and sigh,
And every moment flutters by.
The scent of magic fills the air,
A symphony beyond compare.

As dawn chases the night away,
Fading dreams from yesterday.
Yet in hearts, the echoes stay,
Whispers of faery, forever play.

Glimmers of Joy in the Enchanted Hollow

In the hollow where laughter springs,
Magic dances on fluttering wings.
Glimmers of joy in every hue,
Invite the heart to start anew.

Bright blossoms bloom in radiant glow,
Each petal speaks what hearts will know.
Flowing rivers weave its song,
A melody where dreams belong.

Through emerald canopies, the light,
Drips down softly, pure and bright.
Filling the world with gleaming gold,
Stories of wonders yet untold.

Time drips slow, a droplet's fall,
Echoing laughter, a sweet enthrall.
In the silence, magic weaves,
Binding hearts, like autumn leaves.

As twilight wraps the day in bliss,
Every moment seems to kiss.
In this hollow, joy endures,
A haven where the soul assures.

Empyrean Echoes in the Glade

In the hush of twilight's grace,
Whispers weave beneath the trees,
Stars awaken, soft and bright,
Casting dreams like gentle breeze.

Moonlit shadows softly dance,
Nature's tune, a serenade,
Each flicker holds a story dear,
In this enchanted, timeless glade.

Crickets sing their nightly hymn,
Underneath the silver sky,
Echoes chirp through fragrant air,
Where secrets of the wild lie.

In the heart of emerald night,
Magic lingers, pure and true,
Every step, a world anew,
As the glade reveals its light.

Upon the breeze, sweet scents arise,
Petals whisper, softly curl,
Here in dreams, our spirits soar,
In this haven, magic swirls.

Ethereal Patterns in Night's Veil

Night drapes softly, a velvet cloak,
Stars embroider tales above,
Moonlight spills a shimmering glow,
Nature breathes in peace and love.

Wisps of fog curl, coil, and sway,
Dancing in the misty air,
Each shadow holds an ancient joke,
Whispers of a world so rare.

Crimson blooms beneath the sky,
Glisten with a dewy sheen,
As night unveils its silent art,
In patterns soft and unseen.

Glimmers twine, like threads of fate,
Hushed, the world begins to dream,
Celestial paths in swirling light,
Night weaves wonders, flickering beam.

Every breath, a spell profound,
In this starlit tapestry,
With every heartbeat, echoes sound,
Of love's soft, ethereal decree.

Flickering Glimmers of Enchantment

From bramble thickets, secrets spill,
A flicker calls the night to play,
Softly glimmers, thoughts entwined,
In the woodlands where fairies stray.

Each lantern glows, a guiding light,
Winding paths where whispers lie,
Nature's magic stirs the air,
As dreams of old in shadows sigh.

Moonbeams dance on rippling streams,
Painting ripples, silver bright,
Every flicker, each glimmer's glance,
Unlocks the heart of the night.

Through the trees, enchantments flow,
Threads of gold in twilight's seam,
Stories told in quiet sighs,
Where reality meets the dream.

In the hush, a promise waits,
Magic whispers, soft and true,
Each glimmer leads to new worlds found,
In enchanting realms, we pursue.

Dreamspun Trails of the Woodlands

Through tangled roots and whispered lanes,
The woodland calls, a siren's song,
Each step reveals a hidden world,
Where all the dreamers, they belong.

Beneath the boughs, where shadows play,
Spirits dance on silver beams,
In the hush, the heartbeats blend,
With starlit paths and woven dreams.

Ferns unfurl like secrets shared,
Mossy carpets cradle feet,
Every turn, a new delight,
In this enchanted, wild retreat.

From twilight's arms, the echoes swell,
A symphony of night's embrace,
Guiding us through whispers clear,
To seek the magic, find our place.

In the forest's pulse, we find our way,
Through winding trails, the heart takes flight,
With every sorrow, joy awakes,
Dreamspun paths lead to the light.

Whispers in the Gossamer Woods

In the heart where the silence sings,
Beneath the boughs where the soft wind clings,
Secrets weave through the tangled leaves,
A hush enfolds what the forest believes.

Dewdrops glisten like pearls on grass,
Eyes of wisdom on creatures that pass,
Stories linger in each shadow cast,
Echoes of dreams in the moments past.

Glimmers dance through the twilight air,
Faint as wishes, yet bright and rare,
Nature's whispers, a soothing balm,
Stirring the soul, enfolding calm.

If you listen with heart, wide and free,
You'll find the magic that's meant to be,
For in each rustle and gentle sigh,
Resides the truth of the forest's cry.

Here, where the light and shadows meet,
Every turn holds a tale bittersweet,
So wander softly, let your thoughts flow,
In gossamer woods where the wonders glow.

Luminous Threads of Enchantment

In a realm where the stars weave bright,
Threads of magic spin through the night,
Illuminating paths with a golden hue,
Every heartbeat brings wonders anew.

Mysteries dance in the moonlight's gaze,
Casting dreams through the delicate haze,
A tapestry woven with hope and desire,
Each glimmer ignites an everlasting fire.

Whispers flutter on wings of the breeze,
Carried along through the swaying trees,
The world awakens as shadows depart,
Embracing the glow that ignites every heart.

Feel the pull of the luminous threads,
In every sigh where the magic spreads,
Catch the glow in the corners of time,
Where reality melds with the rhythm of rhyme.

For every moment alive with delight,
Is stitched with enchantment, a wondrous sight,
So follow the gleam, let your spirit soar,
In the luminous web that invites you to explore.

Elfin Dreams in Twilight's Embrace

Beneath the veil of the twilight's hue,
Elfin dreams whisper soft and true,
With laughter that dances on silence unseen,
In every glade where the faeries convene.

Crickets chirp in the fading light,
Painting the world in the colors of night,
Each flicker of fireflies, a secret shared,
A tapestry woven with wishes declared.

A crown of stars on the night sky's head,
Guiding the way where the gentle tread,
For those who believe in the magic of ways,
Will find their hearts set ablaze.

In the embrace of shadows, a murmur of peace,
Elfin laughter that will never cease,
Hold your breath as the twilight sings,
And feel the joy that the night often brings.

With the dawn, these dreams will take flight,
So close your eyes and hold on tight,
For elfin whispers in twilight time,
Are the echoes of a world sublime.

Flickering Shadows of the Moonlit Glade

In a glade where the silver beams fall,
Shadows dance on the ancient wall,
Each flicker and sway, a tender brush,
Woven in stories that time won't hush.

Moonlight spills like a gentle song,
Enchanting all who have wandered along,
A melody sweet as a distant chime,
Bringing the past to life, sublime.

Through rustling leaves, enchantments glide,
In the heart of the night, there's magic inside,
Every creature, a tale to share,
In flickering shadows, none can compare.

As owls call softly from branches above,
The night wraps the world in a mantle of love,
Embracing the dreams that flourish and grow,
In the moonlit glade where the wonders flow.

So linger awhile in the silvery glow,
Let the shadows illuminate the path you know,
For in the stillness of this whispered night,
Lies the heart of magic, eternally bright.

Ethereal Glow of the Verdant Realm

In a grove where shadows dwell,
A luminescent tale does swell,
Leaves of emerald, whispers bright,
Glow in the hush of fading light.

Crystal streams weave through the glen,
Spilling secrets time and again,
While ancient trees in silence stand,
Guarding dreams of the fairyland.

Mists arise in swirling dance,
Hiding wonders in their trance,
Starry eyes of creatures peek,
In the heart, where magic speaks.

Petals soft as silken sighs,
Beneath the shroud of twilight skies,
A tapestry of warmth and lore,
The verdant realm, forevermore.

In this place where spirits tread,
With each step, enchantment spread,
Ethereal glow, a gentle balm,
Whispers of peace, forever calm.

Wanderings in the Whispering Thicket

Through the thicket, shadows weave,
In every rustle, tales believe,
Moonlight drapes the worn path bright,
Leading hearts through endless night.

Creeping vines and brambles thick,
Hold the stories, old and slick,
Each breath carries echoes deep,
Wanderers lose themselves in sleep.

Ferns unfurl beneath the stars,
Guided by the softest tars,
Flitting fireflies mark the way,
In their glow, the night turns day.

Here, the owls softly call,
Ancient guardians of the thrall,
With every flap of feathered grace,
They cradle secrets of this place.

Wanderings weave through dark and light,
In the whispering thicket's might,
A dance of wonder, a fleeting spark,
As dreams take flight in the dark.

Fables Carried on Moonlit Breezes

Beneath the gaze of Luna's prize,
Fables stir in midnight skies,
Carried forth on gentle streams,
Where every whisper becomes dreams.

Secrets tread on silken air,
Lifting tales of joy and care,
As shadows stretch and twirl anew,
Fables born of stars' soft dew.

In the hush, a voice does call,
Echoing where nightingales fall,
Their harmonies blend with the trees,
Carrying myths on moonlit breeze.

Each story hums in soothing tones,
A symphony of ancient bones,
Where laughter lingers, worries cease,
In the night's embrace, find peace.

Fables glimmer, tales away,
In the night, they long to play,
With hearts entwined in magic's breath,
Life unfolds beyond all death.

Tales of Enchantment from the Forest Floor

Where the forest floor does gleam,
Tales awaken from a dream,
Mossy carpets cradle lore,
Each step uncovers mysteries more.

Beneath the boughs, a story stirs,
In the rustle, magic purrs,
Gathered whispers in the breeze,
With every heartbeat, nature sees.

Petals scatter in joyful flight,
Painting paths in morning light,
While mushrooms dance by old oak's side,
Guarding secrets they abide.

Every creature shares a song,
Tales of courage, brave and strong,
From buzzing bees to skittering mice,
In unity, they share the spice.

With every tale, the forest breathes,
A tapestry of woven leaves,
In each echo, life restores,
Tales of enchantment on the shores.

www.ingramcontent.com/pod-product-compliance
Ingram Content Group UK Ltd.
Pitfield, Milton Keynes, MK11 3LW, UK
UKHW021421220125
4239UKWH00007B/175